Philosophy about American Power and Greatness

Philosophy about American Power and Greatness

Dr. François Adja Assemien

THE REGENCY
PUBLISHERS

Copyright © 2022 by Dr. François Adja Assemien.

All rights reserved. No part of this book may be reproduced in any form or by any electronic or mechanical means, including information storage and retrieval systems, without permission in writing from the author and publisher, except by reviewers, who may quote brief passages in a review.

ISBN: 978-1-958517-98-7 (Paperback Edition)
ISBN: 978-1-958517-99-4 (Hardcover Edition)
ISBN: 978-1-958517-97-0 (E-book Edition)

Book Ordering Information

The Regency Publishers, US
521 5th Ave 17th floor NY, NY10175
Phone Number: (315)537-3088 ext 1007
Email: info@theregencypublishers.com
www.theregencypublishers.com

Printed in the United States of America

Contents

From The Same Author v
Introduction vii

First Part: Man according to the American vision

Chapitre 1 : The Nature of man 1
Chapitre 2 : America and others 4
Chapitre 3 : Americans and Existence 9

Second Part: The American spirit

Chapitre 1 : Americans and thought - existence 15
Chapitre 2 : Americans and action 19
Chapitre 3 : From life to existence: a dangerous journey 24
Conclusion 27
Book Summary 31
Author 'S Biography 33

From The Same Author

The Golden Rules of Personal Happiness, Success, Health and Salvation, Edilivre, 2016
Introduction to philocure, essay, Edilivre, 2016
The African Rebels, novel, Edilivre, 2016
Forbidden Africa, novel, Edilivre, 2016
The way of living in America, guide, Edilivre, 2019
Président Donald Trump et les Africains, essai, Edilivre, 2020
The World is worth nothing, essay, Edilivre, 2016
Côte d'Ivoire hurts, essay, Edilivre, 2018
Moral and spiritual education, Edilivre, 2016
The African Consciousness, essay, Edilivre, 2016
Electoral Code, novel, Black Stars, 1995
Portrait of the good and the bad voter, of the good and the bad candidate, essay, Black stars, 2000
The Eleven evils of Côte d'Ivoire, essay, Afro-Star, 2005
Côte d'Ivoire against its foreigners, essay, Black Stars, 2002
The African Guide to Philosophy, Humanities and Humanism, Black Stars, 1985
Political thought to save Ivory Coast, essay, Afro-Star, 2003
Afrocratism, essay, Afro-Star, 1992
Thomas Sankara as Thomas More and Socrates, essay, Ouagadougou, 2020
Ahikaba, novel, Mary Bro Foundation Publishing, London, 2018
Let's save humanity and life, essay, Global Summit House, 2020

The Current slavery in Africa, essay, Global Summit House, 2020
Corona virus, essay, Global Summit House, 2020.

Introduction

I write this book because I am a philosopher. And I'm writing it to show the world the laws of development and potency. I am speaking particularly to weak, poor, underdeveloped countries. **Philosophy about American Power** is their breviary, their viaticum, their vademecum. This book is a school of thought and action. It guides the countries which are in search of development and power in all directions. It shows them what to do. It puts them in the path of power. All nations that are serious about their development and power have an interest in knowing the laws of action and thought that are taught here. It is an imperative duty for them. They must know the energizing and transforming thoughts. They must absolutely follow them, respect them, apply them. We have studied and observed America to discover the principles, rules or laws of gigantism and power. America is a school for the rest of the world, especially for the third world.

It is good to know that being weak, underdeveloped, less developed is not inevitable. This can be explained objectively. It is simply the result of ignorance, of a negative attitude of mind and of a toxic mentality that are diametrically opposed to American mentality. America created its gigantic power and development from its aristocratic, existentialist, voluntarist, pragmatic, optimistic mentality. We can call this work: The American Philosophy of Man, of the World and of Existence. This philosophy is regulating, energizing and composite. It is complex. It is made up of absolute and boundless optimism with regard to man, humanist triumphalism, pragmatism, tragic voluntarism, superhumanism, scientism (absolute faith in science, in technology), Nietzschean elitism or aristocratism, Cartesian rationalism.

According to this philosophy, impossibility is possible for man. American man is ontologically and axiologically conceived as unlimited and without weakness. He is conceived as omnipotent, omniscient and omnipresent. He manifests the divine virtues and attributes. He is transcendent. This philosophy shows how man should think, how he should act and how he should exist. It gives absolute strength and power to the individual to fight, to struggle, to surpass himself and to dominate the world. It shows what the power of will, of mind, of Reason, of intelligence can do in the world. This philosophy teaches men that the fact of living must consist in believing in oneself as one believes in God and in taking oneself for God. Believing in God must mean that one is God. It is more reasonable, more interesting, more important and more profitable. So we must say, like Nietzsche, that God is dead and that he is replaced by man on earth. Man becomes de facto superhuman. He is divine and capable of anything. He can do anything. He just has to trust himself completely. Hence the American expression: "You can. Just do it "(you can do anything. You just have to want to act). This is the responsibility of each man who is really God but who ignores himself as such . From now on , man must become aware of his nature as God. He's like a sleeping God. He must wake up , manifest his creative or divine power to himself and to the world. He must reveal himself and demonstrate that he is perfect. Thus each American-God has the sacred duty to hoist the American flag very high in the sky, above the earth, by his exceptional dynamism, by his heroism, by his superhuman strength and intelligence.

First Part:

Man according to the American vision

Chapter 1

The Nature of man

What is man? Here, we expose the idea that Americans have about themselves (their Americanity) and about man in general as an ideal or a project to be realized. Who is American? That is the individual who was born in America, who grew up in America, who lives in America, who was educated in America. To answer this ontological and axiological question, we have recourse to human sciences and classical philosophy. Let us therefore question philosophers like Hegel, Sartre, Marx, Nietzsche and others who define man. For Hegel, the distinctive mark of man is his self-awareness. Man is spirit. He is spiritual. Man is a subject who thinks of himself and who thinks about the world and things. Spirit fundamentally characterizes man. Indeed, man is particularized or distinguished by the fact that he thinks himself, separates himself from nature, recreates himself through culture, civilization (science, technology, art, religion, morals, law, politics, economy). Man is above all a cultural product. He is the result of his own activity, of the work he does on himself, that is to say his creativity. He is an artificial being. This is what uplifts him, makes him great, powerful and happy. This is exactly what the Americans, who are world champions in science, technique and technology, do. Thus they dominate, modify, transform nature. René Descartes said in the 17th century that science and technology would make of man as master and owner of nature. This is verifiable today in America. That is the greatness of America.

Hegel said that man is a being in and for himself, that he exists for himself. Man is self-aware. He is the author or agent of history, of his history. Americans are authors of their history. They created their superb civilization. They made themselves as Americans. Indeed, man is self-made. He is an artificial being. He is a free subject. He is both in nature and outside of nature by the fact that he is a creative spirit. Hegel thus correctly defines the typical American. Jean-Paul Sartre joins Hegel on this ground. In fact, for him too, man is that being in whom existence precedes essence. Sartre says that man is first and then defines himself by his choices and his actions. Man is freedom. He must define himself and invent himself. It is as it is. There is no human nature prefabricated by God. There is no God to design it. Man is nothing other than what he makes himself. He is fully responsible for what he is. He cannot take refuge behind any determinism or fatalism. He chooses his life and the values that guide him in his existence. The individual cannot not choose. He is doomed to choose. He is nothing other than his project. He only exists to the extent that he realizes himself.

Nietzsche defines American man even better. Better still, the American is Nietzsche's perfect hero. Indeed, the Nietzschean concept of superman corresponds ontologically and axiologically to the typical American. Anthropologically, it is the real American. American is a being who likes to struggle, to work, to create and to **surpass himself** . Now Nietzsche's superman is the man who surpasses himself and transcends man. So American is Nietzschean superman. American is a man who has transcended himself, who has become what he is or a giant. American is a traveler. He started from point A (man) to arrive at point B (superman). Nietzsche says: "Man is a bridge, a crossover towards the superhuman". The superhuman is an absolute lifelong fighter on earth and elsewhere. American man has arrived on the moon. And it evolves towards the other planets. In every man there is an infinity of possible things or qualities which need to be realized or actualized. Nietzsche's message invites humans to realize the infinite possibilities that are in them, that is to say to go from man to superman ". Man is a rope stretched between the beast and the superman, a rope above an abyss "(**Thus spoke Zarathustra**). Americans came out of man as a general envelope and progressed, evolved. They have developed. It is this struggle that we call **existence** . "Man is a being who produces, who materially creates his life to satisfy his basic needs", Karl Marx tells us. This is verifiable in America.

Chapter 2

America and others

America is fighting. It unfolds in the universe . It has become an unparalleled giant. Its relationships with others are based on self-assertion, on the will to power. This is symbolized by the eagle that appears on its national seal. Indeed, this majestic and charismatic bird flies very high and powerfully in the air. It reigns in the air. Its hooked beak and very sharp claws make it formidable and irresistible in combat. So this symbol reflects the strength, dominance and victory of America over others (nature, universe, humanity) . Indeed, America explores, exploits and dominates earth and universe thanks to its incomparable and compelling scientific, technological, economic and military power. René Descartes did not lie: "Science and technology would make man as master and owner of nature", he said . America transforms nature into an artificial environment, very beautiful and very pleasant to inhabit. It plants trees and herbs made by itself there. It maintains waters and protects wild animals. It coexists harmoniously with flora and fauna. It punishes anyone who allows himself to attack and destroy the elements of nature. For example, killing wild animals, catching fish, destroying trees.

The Americans have absolute faith in themselves. As much as they believe in God, the creator, protector, savior, ruler of the universe, so much they believe in themselves as exceptional beings. They believe in their intrinsic abilities, in their paradigms and in their values and virtues such as courage, valor, bravery, intelligence, Reason, will, strength, power, ingenuity, creativity, imagination. They have given themselves two strong symbols that guide them: eagle and star. These two elements express the power and the light which they possess in superabundance. This allowed them to create a paradise on earth. So they reach all the glorious heights. They tear off laurels everywhere. They won independence, sovereignty over England and happiness. So for Americans, everything is possible to America (you can. Just do it). The brand new US President, Joseph R. Biden Jr. said: "I truly believe there is nothing we can't do as a nation, as long as we do it together". He thus displays optimism and voluntarism. He translates his faith in union, in discipline and in work. The impossible is only for other countries which live without existing. These countries have no philosophy for their power, their progress and their development. They ignore the law of greatness, of gigantism. They ignore the law of American gigantism which can be summed up by the formula: "you can. Just do it ". However, it is this law which guides and encourages all entrepreneurs, all economic operators, all political actors, all sportsmen, all engineers, all artists, researchers, scientists, thinkers, writers, in short, everyone in America.

The fifty stars of the American federal flag mean for us: union, discipline, work. It is a major ideological asset as a mobilizing, regulating and revolutionary symbolism. It is the royal path of American progress, omnipotence and gigantism. It reflects the supreme dream and ideal of Americans. The United States of America is a homogeneous, original and unique political entity in the world. This political entity is founded on solidarity, discipline and action. Discipline is enlightened citizenship and patriotism. This consists for the Americans in accepting to live together, in solidarity, under the same authority, under the same constraints, the same laws and the same federal constitution. "Obedience to the law that we have prescribed is freedom," says Jean-Jacques Rousseau. Americans are united by mind, by heart, by reason and by wisdom. Union is popular concord and consensus around common ideals, values and goals. The colors appearing in the American federal flag have a deep and salutary meaning. They support and translate the vision or philosophy of American gigantism. White means purity and innocence as the ideals that channel Americans. Red expresses the exceptional bravery and courage or heroism that characterizes Americans. As for blue, it symbolizes the ideal of egalitarian and distributive justice which maintains America in happiness, peace, security, stability, understanding, union, concord, communion, greatness.

Omnipotence is infinite, absolute and all-out power. It is reflected in the political, economic, cultural, military, scientific and technological supremacy achieved thanks to the work, the creativity, the genius of the Americans. Very hard, very intensive and very rational work is what gives Americans more value and happiness. It is because of this that Americans are above all the other peoples of the world. You should know that work has a completely different function and a whole other interest for Americans. It is through it, in fact, that Americans discover themselves as such, realize themselves and define man. Elsewhere, work is seen very negatively as a divine punishment and curse (the famous Original Sin of Christians). In America, work is seen as a very positive value. It is thanks to it that Americans realize their divine nature, their superhumanity, their transcendence. Indeed, work allows Americans to measure and exploit to the maximum the human capacities, to test the strength, the value, the creative genius, the talents, the inventiveness of each man. Work then represents a barometer, a Roberval balance and a thermometer. Through work, we know that man has unlimited, extraordinary and inexhaustible strengths and capacities. Human intelligence, imagination, memory, Reason, will and power are limitless and inexhaustible. The working individual uses only a very small part of these human resources and qualities. The employers who know this then demand from the workers a maximum of effort and productivity. Bosses ask their employees to work tirelessly and to give their best and most of themselves for the growing happiness, success and prosperity of their businesses. And very often without adequate compensation on their part, without fair remuneration for workers. Workers are asked not to spare their capacities and their strength. They are told that they can do anything, that there is nothing impossible for man (You can. Just do it). Impossible is not American. Laziness, fatigue, fear, cowardice, cheating, neglect and mediocrity are not accepted. This is strictly prohibited and repressed by American employers.

The aristocratic spirit, the mentality of the superman, the cult of infinite excellence, of limitless perfection are imposed on all in a climate of ruthless and deadly competition. Good citizenship and patriotism are measured by their ability to apply these virtues at work and to pay income taxes to their local state and to the federal state. You are considered an infallible and divine being. You are therefore not entitled to error or fault. So all workers must fight to death or surpass themselves. They are in fierce competition with each other. The weak and the mediocre are eliminated, dismissed without mercy in the name of the productivity that we want to increase and in the name of maximum profit. Only the best, the strongest, the excellent can continue to work. Any favoritism, any laxity, any nepotism and any cheating are very severely punished. Complacency, corruption, negligence, levity, lies, dishonesty and injustice are not American. They have no right to exist in America. America is fighting them to death. This is very evident in the workplace in America. Gigantism goes with elitism and selectivism. It demands extreme severity and rigor. It is based on a fierce discipline of a military nature. So it is very easy to lose your job and very difficult to keep it for a long time. American worker is subject to constant harsh criticism and very strict daily control. He is evaluated and judged at all times (it is called in English *survey*). He must be flawless and in excellence . We don't need humans but superhumans or machines to work perfectly. Superhumans or machines are perfect, tireless, infallible, very profitable. Only geniuses, superhumans and champions have to work. To each according to his merit, his competence, his talents and his conduct. *You can. Just do it. Do your best* . **Be the best ever** . This is the law of American gigantism or greatness.

Chapter 3

Americans and Existence

The fact of existing is to strive to improve and save one's life. It consists of fighting against all hostile, harmful forces, against nature and universe. Existence is life channeled, organized, planned and thought-oriented towards a goal, an ideal. In this sense, animals and things do not exist. Only man exists because he thinks about his life and transforms it. He invents, chooses the means and conditions of his life. He is active while animals and things are passive, conforming to the laws of nature and universe. How do Americans fight and struggle for existence? How do they act on their life and natural things, in order to access existence? American existence is driven by several philosophical theories: voluntarism, rationalism, superhumanism, liberalism, pragmatism, scientism, optimism, existentialism. According to Aristotle, the goal of life is happiness. This happiness is won through struggle (existence). Americans spend their life in a fierce struggle for happiness. What is this happiness that men aim for? Happiness is the result of the liberating and salutary struggle. It is the condition or state of one who has come out of hardship, suffering, bondage, misery, poverty and misfortune. In other words, existence is the best possible quality of living (Paradise). Happiness is the just reward of heroes, champions, victors, masters. It is the fruit of conquest, of victory. It therefore presupposes struggle, war. This is why it is not accessible to the weak, the vanquished, the dominated, the slaves. It is the prerogative or monopoly of the strong, the powerful, the triumphant. The winners are in joy. They are happy. They enjoy their **power.** How about the vanquished? Where is their joy or the source of their joy? Can they feel the joy of the overcomers? No. They are unhappy. There is no joy or pride to be derived from helplessness, defeat, shame, failure, weakness, unhappiness. This is obvious.

Existence is an act of force, of power. It is based on the will to power. It is obtained after getting rid of all the prejudices of vulgar, ascetic, religious morality. It is the conquerors alone who make the laws of this world. They impose their will on the vanquished. Laws are from the dominators and not from the dominated. Kings and Presidents make laws because they are powerful. God makes laws because he is omnipotent. Masters make laws. A father makes laws. But slaves and children make no law. They are dominated. There are political, economic, religious, moral, intellectual or ideological rulers. They rule over humanity. They rule the world by their thoughts or by their actions. They hold the secrets of happiness. It is, for example, cunning, intelligence, imagination, intellectual, spiritual, psychological, physical power. So there are several categories of men in the world. There are the **masters** (the powerful, the rulers, the lions), the **slaves** (the weak, the ruled, the sheep) and the **rebels** . The rebels are the slaves who fight to free themselves from domination, from servitude. They are revolutionaries, awakening consciousness. Indeed, a slave can free himself by struggle, by his bravery, his courage, his fearlessness, his daring. He can become a master. The former master can in turn become a slave. Any reversal of the situation or condition of a person or a group is possible in the ever-evolving world, in constant movement. A king can become a beggar and a beggar can become a king. People's social and political positions are interchangeable. Nothing is final, stable or eternal. Everything is contingent, evanescent, accidental, occasional, ephemeral on earth. This is the only constant. It is the law of existence or the law of the will to power.

To exist etymologically means to evolve, progress, develop, assert oneself, become other, better, powerful. It is coming out of a lower state (or condition) into a higher, better state. Thus to exist is opposed to living. Indeed, the act of living is natural, animal. Life is given to every man free of charge by the act of procreation. But after his birth, man builds himself and creates his story. He becomes what he chooses to be. He makes himself a place of master or slave. Either he is subject to the domination of others or he imposes himself on others as king. Existence is an act that creates values. It is an aristocratic fight. It is the noble struggle that creates great men, superior men. It is the combat which makes pass from the status of slave, of sheep, to the status of master, of lion. If you are a slave, it means that you are not struggling. Because the fight transforms the wrestler, makes him evolve, progress. Americans struggle a lot. And they have become the masters of the world. Who were their ancestors? They were Europeans, especially the British or the English, who were **transformed** into Americans through struggle. Thus they created a force and a civilization superior to that of their country of origin, England. They fought and transcended England, its values and its archaic (old school) paradigms. America is a **new** world, a **new** England, **another** England (New England). The new English or the English overseas are omnipotent, omniscient, omnipresent. They are demigods. They are the masters of the world. They have won victories and victories over themselves, over other peoples and especially over the English monarchy, over Queen Elizabeth. They are irresistible and incomparable to other peoples. They have given themselves all the means to progress and to always be masters. They have confidence in themselves. They cultivated **optimism** (you can. Just do it), **liberalism** , **scientism** (absolute faith in science-technology), **voluntarism** (the will to power, domination), **pragmatism** (the sense of efficiency, creative effort, success, realism, dynamism), **rationalism** (faith in Reason). The whole of America is a mathematical, logical, scientific construction. In there, everything is calculated, measured. The Americans have developed machinery to the limit. American life is fully mechanized, computerized and electronic. Everything here relies on the use of intelligent machines, sophisticated and more efficient than humans. So Americans don't just live like animals, they really exist. They have transcended their first condition, animal and human, to reach superhumanity and the rank of God. In America, we see that God is really **dead** and that he is replaced on earth by reasonably materialistic men. In America, we can feel the influence of two great proactive and existentialist thinkers: Nietzsche and Jean-Paul Sartre. Both teach the transcendence of man, super humanism, absolute optimism with regard to man, voluntarism. We retain from these two philosophers that man is only what he makes himself or the product of his will, of his Reason. We remember that man is absolutely responsible for his existence because that is his creation. We remember that man is spirit, free, transcendent. Man invents himself.

Second Part:

The American spirit

Chapter 1

Americans and thought - existence

According to René Descartes, Reason is the best shared thing in the world. If this is true, let us recognize that Americans have received more Reason than other peoples. They received the lion's share, that is to say the largest share. Descartes defines man as the thinking being (res cogitans in Latin). He says he is because he **thinks** . "Cogito ergo sum" (I think therefore I am). The worthy and responsible man is the one who is conscious of himself, who thinks rationally, philosophically, mathematically, scientifically. Thus he, Descartes, as a philosopher, undertook to think, to demolish and to rebuild all the edifice of knowledge built by others that he finds doubtful, not certain (methodological skepticism). Descartes thus developed a new morals (morals by provision), a new metaphysics based on the affirmation of the existence of God. He shows that to think is to recreate, to doubt any thought received, to question things, to criticize them. It's about bringing out the new, the best. This is an imperative duty and an absolute necessity for humanity in search of happiness, salvation, power, progress. Thus cartesianism (or the cartesian spirit) favored the development and elevation of America. It is in this same way that Nietzsche and Sartre also contributed to the rise of America. Man is spirit, thinking substance, "res cogitans" (thinking thing in Latin). He is a rope stretched between the animal and the superman (Nietzsche). He is freedom (Sartre). It is a being who produces, materially creates his life to satisfy his basic needs (Karl Marx). All of this appears to be unique to Americans (their character). Americans embody and express the progressive and revolutionary philosophy ordered to the rebirth and the power of men, peoples and nations.

Life determines consciousness and consciousness determines life. This shows the capital importance of thought. What is the primary purpose of thought? It is happiness of men. It is the good of humanity. So thinking consists in producing happy, beneficent, salutary ideas. To think is to reconstruct things given by nature. To think is to improve life, to promote progress and development, enrich and maintain civilization, to take a step back from animals and other beings in nature. This fight is called EXISTENCE. To think is to exist. "Cogito ergo sum". To think is to bring things into being. To thing is to create, to invent a new, better or superior world. Animals and things don't think. They are moved by natural laws. They are limited and frozen in their original nature. They cannot create anything, invent anything, improve their life. They do not exist. They are natural. As for man, he is artificial because he is imaginative, intelligent, endowed with Reason. He thinks, dreams and makes plans. This makes him powerful, happy, prosperous, master and owner of nature. America's power, prosperity and development were created by English adventurers who were persecuted in their country. Today, persecuting England is dominated by America. It cannot be compared to America. England is archaic, mediocre and inferior to America it created from scratch. America is the fruit of mind or thought. To think is to free oneself from suffering, from evil, from nature, from universe. It is to be reborn, to transform (to exist). People who do not think or who kill their thinkers are wrong. They condemn themselves to weakness, mediocrity, impotence. It is their greatest misfortune. They refrain from any possibility of evolving, prospering, progressing, developing. They regress, fall into decay. They remain small, dominated, crushed, enslaved by peoples who think, who create, who aim very high, very far. The world and happiness belong to those who think. The present and the future belong to the thinking, calculating, ambitious people. So African peoples who do not think, who persecute and kill their thinkers, their heroes, their visionaries and their revolutionaries stagnate. They are crushed, humiliated, enslaved, colonized and reduced to things and their simplest expression.

To think is above all to seek, find or create the necessary means of one's life (happiness, security, power, peace, comfort, health). Without thought, there is no happiness, no salvation, no possibility of a dignified and genuine human life. Without thought, one is assimilated to beast and object. The highest and noblest thought that separates man from things and beasts is **concept** thought (the conceptualization of things and the world) . It is the work of philosophers and scientists. It is the source of history and civilization. It puts man above instinctive, natural and animal life. It is characteristic of human being who thinks and **speaks**. Animal did not create history or civilization. It didn't do these two things because it doesn't have access to Reason or conceptual intelligence. It cannot be a philosopher, scientist, engineer ... But if Reason is the thing best shared with humans, it must be recognized that all humans do not manifest it in the same way or to the same degree. It is one thing to have Reason and it is another to know how to use it for one's salvation. There is a waste of Reason among many people, among certain peoples. For example, Africans today do not use their Reason in a sufficient or beneficial way. Hence their sufferings, their miseries and their multiple misfortunes. It pits Africa against America. America is indeed very rational, very calculating. It is created and populated by men who think rationally, methodically, skillfully, who think a lot and deeply. America is the work of people who have set themselves a glorious goal (a very great vision) and who have given themselves the adequate means to achieve this goal (all-out gigantism). Descartes, the father of "cogito ergo sum", would he have been born for America, to help Americans? What is very certain, the greatest Cartesians, that is to say the thinkers or calculators, are Americans. The true Cartesians are those who created American gigantism by their calculations, their reflections, their scientific and philosophical talents or skills. I therefore think I am American. I therefore think I am a giant. I therefore think I am the master and possessor of earth. I therefore think I am God. Paraphrasing Descartes: God is perfect. So it necessarily exists. Because if it lacked the quality of existence, it would not be perfect. Americans therefore think they exist. They are perfect, they are God. Whoever knows America knows Heaven. Whoever knows America knows the creative power of God. He knows the omnipotence of God. Homo Americanus Deus est.

Chapter 2

Americans and action

Henri Bergson said: "We must act as a man of thought and think as a man of action". By this chiasmus, this philosopher shows that action must go hand in hand with thought or else that these two things are inseparable and complementary. The thinker must act, that is to say realize his ideas in the world. An abstract thought, cut off from the real or unrealizable has no value (pragmatism). Theory without practice is futile and practice without theory is blind. We must therefore combine these two things to make them fruitful, effective and useful. This is as valid in science (theory and experience) as in politics and morals (ideology and politico-union struggle). In the same sense and in epistemology, Emmanuel Kant maintains that: " Intutions without concepts are blind and concepts without intutions are empty". Marxist philosophers and all the great political revolutionaries and trade unionists agree in recognizing this truth according to which we must always unite thought to action in order to obtain maximum efficiency, to make thought and action fruitful, creative.

Action is understood here as struggle, combat, political, social, economic, cultural commitment aimed at changing, correcting, improving things in the world. Action is the existential struggle based on the desire for progress, power, happiness. Without action there is no existence. Existence means struggle, action. Action is a precious attribute of the American people. It is thinks to action (work, battle) that Americans have distinguished themselves and outclassed all other peoples on earth. It is thanks to action dialectically linked to thought that they have constituted their supreme power, that they have created their exceptional gigantism and that they are respected and feared by the whole world. Voluntary, ambitious, enlightened action guided by Reason and Consciousness, transforms and improves the life of a wise people. America is the field of experimentation for this theory. America is a school of progress, success, prosperity, victory, gigantism, development, exemplarity. A people who dreams only without acting, without struggling, will remain small, like a big, pitiful and ashamed baby. This people will be the laughing stock of the world, the sum of pain, suffering and misfortune. A country that neither dreams nor acts is a country in danger of death. It is called to disappear from earth. It is impossible for it to live. Its place is the cemetery. This is the proven case of African countries which refrain from dreaming and acting. Thus all ways of dignity, honor, power, greatness, elevation, glory, success, prosperity, development, liberty, emancipation, autonomy, independence and sovereignty remain hermetically closed to them until they wake up.

Man is made to struggle and exist. This is his normal and natural duty according to perspective and voluntarist morals. The concepts of man, people, country, nation are regulatory, perspective, pragmatic. They contain a prospective and aristocratic (Nietzschean) responsibility that man (or a country) must assume or disappear. Man is a project or a projection. He is free. If he does not assume his nature of being free, a fighter, he has resigned. He suppresses himself or falls into the class of inferior, non-free beings like beasts, plants, stones etc. Therefore he does not deserve life or else he survives as a slave or beast of burden. He denied himself. He gave up his nature as a thinker, a wrestler. He has become animal or thing. Each man (or people) chooses his price. He chooses to be king or to be a slave. He chooses to be free or to be dominated, enslaved. All human conditions or social positions are exposed for sale in the world market. And each of us buys the titles, the statutes that he likes. Everyone therefore chooses his fate. Therefore, he must assume it. He deserves everything that happens to him in his life. Compassion, empathy, pity have no value. These Buddhist and Christian sentiments have no reason to exist. They are very absurd. Individual freedom to choose one's status makes everyone responsible for himself. The collective freedom to choose our fate or condition makes all people responsible for themselves. This individual or collective responsibility legitimately causes sanctions that make everyone happy or unhappy. We must exclude here any superstition and any fatality which derive from ignorance or bad faith of men. Gods and other real or supposed forces, as creatures of religion and metaphysics, have nothing to do for or against men. Humans are not created or managed by them. It is humans who create them in their mind and imagination, and in their image, for their various needs and interests. Humans project themselves into things, lend them their qualities, their faults and their feelings (mythologies, fictions). Then they worship them and maintain them cowardly and stupidly. It is a great world comedy and a macabre universal grimace. It is called **illusion.** That is a grotesque, personal or collective lie that functions and thrives everywhere through hypocrisy, cunning, manipulation and mental weakness of each other. It is a very old social, economic, political (domination) and cultural system which reflects the relationship of the shepherds (pastus) to their sheep. This system of self-negation and alienation based on fear is the obvious sign of the greatest weakness and voluntary helplessness of peoples. It is defeatism, pessimism, a lack of self-confidence in the face of existential combat that men refuse. It is a very dangerous headlong rush. Thus the proclamation of the death of the official and world God by the philosopher Nietzsche (iconoclast) constitutes the greatest historical drama. This caused general panic on earth, the greatest despair in the man-slave or sheep. The latter no longer knows where to turn or what saint to turn to. It is truly a disaster or the greatest danger for him. It defeats him, confuses him, and ruins all his hope. Indeed, his last rampart, his last fortress, his only shield, his help and his lifeline are broken in four. So he is now more unhappy than ever. He no longer has any help or an illusory protector. Anguish and dizziness take hold of this great orphan and devour him entirely. The death of God is the most terrible event in the world, in life and in history. Nietzsche is then declared persona non grata, the greatest historical criminal, the worst enemy of the sick, the weak and the sheep who are unable to defend themselves and to be happy without the belief in a saving god that filled them with fatherly love. Nietzsche is liable to the death penalty, he, the sworn and common enemy of the herd, of the decadents, of the reprobates, of the slaves.

It is Nietzsche, the Anti-Christ. He authorizes the killing of God. We, his proud followers, happily celebrate this historic event with Apollo and Dionysus. This is our happiness, our strength, our victory and leaves us the freedom to act with confidence. We only believe in ourselves. We rely absolutely and only on ourselves. Long live the salutary death of the domineering, dictator, illusory God who denies the power, freedom and happiness of man. We proudly occupy its erased place in human mind and memory. We deliver and free all worshipers and prisoners of God. Its so glorious and exceptional attributes like omnipotence, omniscience and omnipresence are rightfully ours. Thus let us redefine man with Nietzsche: "Man is a rope stretched between the beast and the superman". The faith of Americans in God is the way and the instrument of their progress, of their transformation, of their historic revolution. "In God we trust" really means, for us, the absolute faith of Americans in themselves as replacements and images of a dead God. God is in them. God is their **Reason** . It means that they have the values or attributes of God. They are therefore legitimately very confident. Thus they win all their existential battles and in all areas. Nothing limits or stops them. They meet all natural, political, economic, cultural, military challenges etc. They are legitimately very **optimistic** (you can. Just do it), **rationalists** (I think therefore I am American), **pragmatists** (action pays, saves), **existentialists** (existence precedes essence), **scientists** (science and technology has made them the masters and owners of nature and the world). They are proactive. They believe in the transforming power of will, of Reason, of action. This is how they created the most powerful nation and the most beautiful civilization in the world.

Chapter 3

From life to existence: a dangerous journey

Nietzsche said, in **Thus Spoke Zarathustra**, that "Man is a rope stretched between animal and the superman, a rope above an abyss". In other words, humanity is a bridge, a high-risk passage. It is a painful transition to superhumanity. Man must seek his perfection. He must evolve, progress, develop by paying a very heavy price, by undergoing very great pain. Man has to moult. He must make his revolution and metamorphose. It is a perilous but glorious and salutary journey. He must transform his biological and natural condition into existence. Reason, conscience and tragic wisdom have the duty to kill the vulgar man and replace him with the superman. It is a question of passing from the rank of sheep to the rank of lion, of passing from the rank of slave to the rank of master, of replacing God by the superman. Ordinary life is attribute of man. Existence is attribute of superman. Man lives and superman exists. Man has the imperious and supreme duty to become superman. **His ultimate goal is to be a superman**. It is his sovereign task. He must take the path of Deity. He must change his morals. He must take tragic, aristocratic morals and mentality, that is to say the status of bird of prey, of triumphant warrior, of blond beast according to Nietzsche. He must appropriate the three great attributes of God: omnipotence, omnipresence, omniscience. Life made him weak, helpless, a slave, a thing. He must learn to fight all this, to break with this shameful, unworthy, irresponsible status. He has within him the potential ability to change his old habit and put on a new and glorious habit. He can transform himself and become an aristocrat, master, agent of a new history.

There is a superman and a sleeping demigod within us humans. Man must wake them up and make them work for his benefit. He must put them to the fight for his liberation, his rebirth, his progress, his upliftment in all directions, his mental, spiritual, moral, physical, political, economic, cultural development. He must assume and realize his deity, his superhumanity for his happiness and his salvation in the declining world. He must manifest or actualize the will to power that lies dormant in him and dominate the world. He is divine. In him are all the divine virtues of his positive transformation into a superman. America has taken this perilous journey with triumph. It managed to pass from life to existence. Americans have reached the rank of superman. They have made their mental, moral, civilizational revolution. Hence their development and their prodigious, gigantic progress. They've come to the point where they can do anything. This became possible thanks to their will to power. They absolutely believe in themselves, in their unlimited capacity, in their infallibility. They work day and night, at all times. They produce or create all the goods and all the means of their maximum development. They are currently conquering the entire universe. They landed heroically on the moon and are now going to conquer the other planets. They master science and technology far more than any other people in the world. This ensures them all-round victories. Their Cartesian rationalism is a sure and irresistible force. It is an infallible shield, weapon and tool. So the present and the future belong to America. Their leitmotif or slogan ("You can. Just do it ") says it all. This is very expressive and very eloquent vis-à-vis the mentality and the philosophy of the Americans launched in the race for power, for happiness, for omniscience, for omnipotence, for omnipresence. Everything is within their reach: superhumanity, control, domination, mastery of the world.

America was able to pass from life to existence thanks to three operational and regulatory concepts: **union, discipline, work** . These are its central and ideological pillars. Union is the creation of a gigantic, federal state (50 United States). There is no political gigantism without legal, moral, civic, economic rigor. America is a state of law, morals and religion. It exists and functions harmoniously thanks to fervent and exemplary civility and patriotism. America lives its credo (in God we trust). Divine transcendence is its ideal and its virtue. Americans believe they are made in the image of God. Besides, God is dead. They fully assume their divine nature or deity as a sacred heritage . As nothing is impossible with God, nothing is impossible with Americans (you can. Just do it). They won their fight for gigantism and world leadership thanks to their fierce and unwavering will, their relentlessness, their ardor, their intrepidity, their bravery, their heroism. The Nietzschean project of superhumanity is carried out in America. Well done to America!

Conclusion

We have exposed the theoretical or ideological foundations of American gigantism. We hope this will help everyone get to know America better. The lesson that emerges from this work is that one does not become the greatest and the most powerful in the world without doing anything, without dreaming very big and without fighting to the death, without taking risks of all kinds. We sincerely hope that this will help weak, poor, decadent, miserable and unhappy countries to recover, correct themselves and develop. We have dealt with the following questions: What is the secret or the law of American gigantism? In other words: from what does America derive its supreme greatness, its supreme power, its supreme prosperity, its supreme success and its supreme quantitative and qualitative development? Why do other countries not equal America? What sets America apart from other nations? What is the American mindset (or spirit) made of? What is the American vision of life, of existence, of man, of God, of universe, of nature, of the world? What are the philosophies, thoughts and doctrines that have influenced, determined, conditioned the behavior and conduct of Americans? We are far from having exhausted this problem. We do not give peremptory or exhaustive answers to the questions asked. Our answers do not nail everyone's mouth. The other thinkers and researchers (Americanists or Americanologists) have the freedom and the full right to criticize us and to continue this work in their direction and according to their capacities and their intellectual tastes. No one has the absolute truth. Each has his truth, his lie, his error and his illusion. Everyone has his sweet tooth. And this contributes to the progress of thought, to the enrichment of knowledge. It is the condition for being and the reason for living of philosophy and of human, social and moral sciences. **Consensus suppresses philosophy** . No one is supposed to ignore that philosophy has been nourished by controversy and subjectivity since its birth. Philosophical theses have never been apodictic truths. All philosophical discourse is relative and subjective (see Bertrand Russell). Certainty is the tomb of philosophy. It certainly kills philosophy which is a permanent debate. Certainty puts an end to philosophy by transforming it into science. This is true of science itself to a large extent (there is no exact science).

Philosophical truth is comparable to opinion (doxa). Everyone has his opinion of the world. Likewise, each philosopher has his opinion of the world. If our opinion of America is different from the opinions of others, it is very normal. It is not a fault or an evil. Rather, it is the general rule. Didn't Hegel say that each philosopher arises while opposing the others? So is intellectual activity in the world. It is the law of the world of knowledge. Roughly speaking, we have said that America created itself as it is from a psychology or a special attitude of mind which favors the blossoming, progress and all-out development of a people or of a nation. This attitude consists in thinking and believing that **everything is permitted and possible for man** if he trusts himself, if he trusts his Reason (rationalism), his will (voluntarism) and if he acts with power (pragmatism). Indeed, man embodies the absolute perfection and power of God. God is conceived as omnipotent, omniscient, omnipresent. In truth, God is the ideal image or the greatest symbol of man as desired by great philosophers like Nietzsche, Descartes, Sartre and others. God is the sublimation of man, that is to say the final goal that man wants to achieve in his self-realization, in his absolute self-fulfillment through his existential and perfectionist struggle. God is the positive and sublime image of the superior man projected above man by man. It is a creative superstition to beget Nietzsche's superman. To believe in God and to adore God is in reality to believe in man and to adore man as we want him, that is to say the sublimated man . Man must be God. Theistic and deistic religions therefore worship man in truth. They worship the ideal or the perfect man. In God we trust means deeply: we believe in ourselves, as humans, as Americans, enjoying the very glorious virtues and attributes that we attribute to God, the invisible, our sublime creature. God is the greatest regulatory idea that allows us to recreate our world, to free the vulgar man from all bondage, from all domination, from all alienation, from all powerlessness, from all weakness, from all suffering, from all poverty, from all misery and all evil. Elsewhere, in some countries, God is the privileged and most effective instrument which sustains, comforts, consoles the partisans of the least effort, the lazy, the coward, and keeps the weak and the slaves in their infernal situation. In America, it is quite the opposite. So the symbol of God is used differently across the world, either positively or negatively. Nietzsche, the murderer of God, advises us to use it positively,in American style. Let's create and use God wisely, for our greatest happiness and salvation. Let us transform all the countries of the world into Paradise where the good Lord resides. This is the most interesting, the most useful and the most important for humanity. It is for this only that the idea or the ideal of God must be used. Let's do wonders and miracles like God. To God there is nothing impossible. The impossible is to human but not to God that is omnipotent, omniscient and omnipresent. Long live God! Long live the superman! Long live America !

Book Summary

Philosophy about American greatness and power is a very special and beneficial school. It wants to create exceptional men on earth. It aims to create stars and elite peoples that will clear the darkness, remove helplessness, weakness and suffering of this world and help everyone exist gloriously with honor and dignity.

Author's Biography

Dr. François Adja Assemien was born on March 15, 1954 in Côte d'Ivoire (West/Africa). He studied the humanities (Latin and Greek), the social sciences and philosophy. He is graduate in philosophy (PhD) and in sociology (Bachelor's degree). He devoted himself to teaching (philosophy), writing and academic research. He speaks and writes three modern languages: French, English and German.

He is author of several books published in France and the United States of America (novels, essays, short stories, plays) and of several concepts such as Afrocratism, Philocure, Sidarologie, African Consciousness, Aboubou music. He is also an artist, musician, singer, composer and guitarist.

He lives in the United States of America .